By the same author

Little Red Book Series

Little Red Book of Slang-Chat Room Slang

Little Red Book of English Vocabulary Today

Little Red Book of Grammar Made Easy

Little Red Book of English Proverbs

Little Red Book of Prepositions

Little Red Book of Idioms and Phrases

Little Red Book of Euphemisms

Little Red Book of Effective Speaking Skills

Little Red Book of Modern Writing Skills

Little Red Book of Verbal Phrases

Little Red Book of Synonyms

Little Red Book of Antonyms

Little Red Book of Common Errors

Little Red Book of Letter Writing

Little Red Book of Perfect Written English

Little Red Book of Essay Writing

Little Red Book of Word Power

Little Red Book of Spelling

Little Red Book of Language Checklist

Little Red Book of Word Fact

A2Z Book Series

A2Z Quiz Book

A2Z Book of Word Origins

Others

The Book of Fun Facts

The Book of More Fun Facts

The Book of Firsts and Lasts

The Book of Virtues

The Book of Motivation

Read Write Right: Common Errors in English

The Students' Companion

Fun with Riddles

Fun with Numbers

Fun with Maths

FUN
WITH
PUZZLES

TERRY O'BRIEN

RUPA

Published by
Rupa Publications India Pvt. Ltd., 2013
7/16, Ansari Road, Daryaganj
New Delhi 110002

Sales centres:
Allahabad Bengaluru Chennai
Hyderabad Jaipur Kathmandu
Kolkata Mumbai

ISBN: 978-81-291-2383-1

10 9 8 7 6 5 4 3 2 1

The moral right of the author has been asserted.

Typeset in Times New Roman 10/12
by Innovative Processors, New Delhi

Printed at HT Media Ltd., Noida

Acknowledgement

A special thanks to Allen O'Brien, my son,
who assisted me in having fun while
compiling and re-imagining what's
essential for such a book

PREFACE

Mathematics is a part and parcel of everyday life. In fact, one can find curious mathematics in God's creation. Not only does man excel in it, but even a honey comb or a cobweb has mathematical synergy. However, the time has come to rethink our approach to the skills of thinking.

Fun with Puzzles can be fun. And so here comes a book that has tried to turn mathematics into a game with the bottom line being the 3Ls: Love, Laugh and Learn! So let us put on our thinking caps.

Puzzle No. 1

The registration plates of all these cars follow a certain sequence. Can you work out the final number?

CAR-1

CAR- 2

DL-759

UP-8610

CAR-3

CAR- 4

MP-1311

JK- 1614

CAR - 5

Q ?

Puzzle No. 2

SET 1

Out on a Shopping Spree

With ₹15/- in hand: one rupee notes and 20 p. coins, out goes Nikita on a shopping spree. Here goes the surprise: She returns with many one rupee notes as she originally had and as many 20 p. coins as she originally had one rupee notes. She came back with about one third of what she had started out with. Are you stumped?

How much did Nikita spend and exactly how much did she have with her when she started out?

SET 2

Nikita Travels

Nikita was driving from her home to the Zoo. It took her 1 hour and 30 minutes to complete the journey.

After lunch Nikita returned home. She drove for 90 minutes. How come?

Puzzle No. 3

The weight of each person is mentioned below. Select the odd one out?

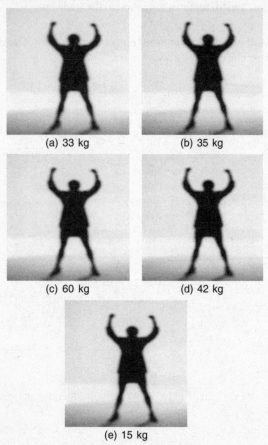

(a) 33 kg

(b) 35 kg

(c) 60 kg

(d) 42 kg

(e) 15 kg

Puzzle No. 4

SET 1

Nikita has a question

Come on Tina, can you name the smallest integer that can be written with two digits?

SET 2

Tina gives it back!

Nikita, name the biggest number that can be written with four 1s?

SET 3

A Problem of Badminton

There are 150 members in Nikita's club. They decided to have a badminton tournament. All the members came forward to play in the game. Every time a member loses a game she was out of the tournament.

There are no ties.

Nikita and Tina wondered if they could tell how many games must be played in order to determine the champion. Can we do so?

Puzzle No. 5

Help Nikita arrange 9 cards in a 3 × 3 matrix. Here are the details:

The cards are of 4 colours: Red, Yellow, Blue, Green.
Note that one red card must be in the first row or second row. 2 green cards should be in the 3rd column. Yellow cards must be in the 3 corners only. Two blue cards must be in the 2nd row. And finally, one green card must be placed in each row. Your time starts now!

Puzzle No. 6

SET 1

How old is Nikita?

Nikita is three years hence multiplied by 3 and from that subtracted three times her age three years ago will give you her exact age.

How old do you think Nikita is?

SET 2

The Puzzle that Nikita asked

Come on Tina - Look at this:

$159 \times 48 = 7632$

Notice this multiplication? Yes, all the nine digits are different. How many other similar numbers can you think of dear Tina?

Puzzle No. 7

Take one letter from each square in order. Set them in a way that you end up making 5 letter words that are names of food items.

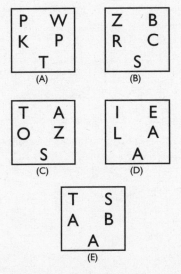

Puzzle No. 8

SET 1

Nikita's writing challenge

Come on Tina: write 1/81 as a repeating decimal—don't be surprised!

SET 2

A scooty is manufactured with 11 parts. In order to make one scooty, you get 1 part as scrap. On the 5th of January, you have 250 such scraps. Now with that amount of scrap, how many scooties can you manufacture?

Puzzle No. 9

Time to find the missing number in this square.

1536	48	96	3
384	192	24	12
768	96	48	6
192	?	12	24

Puzzle No. 10

SET 1

Tina's combination problem

Can you now help Tina combine eight 8s with any other mathematical symbols… except numbers so that they represent exactly 1000?

Feel free to use addition, subtraction and division signs as well as the factorial function along with the Gamma function. Also, you can use the logarithms and the combinatorial symbol.

SET 2

There are five servants. Each get their share of diwali sweets one after the other. Servant 1 gets 1/2 of the total no. of the sweets plus 1/2 of a single sweet. Servant 2, 3, 4, 5 also gets the same. After the fifth one, the total number of sweets remaining are 3. So how many sweets were there initially?

Puzzle No. 11

What can you think of to replace the question mark down there?

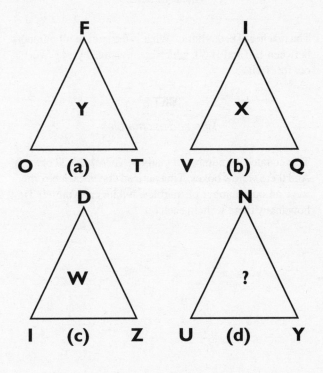

Puzzle No. 12

SET 1

Nikita at school

The teacher asked Nikita, 'What is the sum of all numbers between 100 and 1000, which are divisible by 14?' Work it out for Nikita.

SET 2

Tina and her marbles

Tina counted the number of marbles. There were 27 of them. And there were 4 boxes. Tina noticed that in each box there were an odd number of marbles. Nikita can you tell Tina how many there were in each box?

Puzzle No. 13

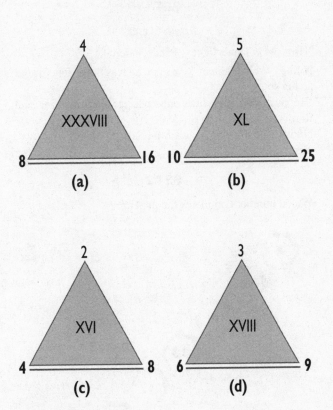

There is one triangle that does not follow the same rule as the other. Which one is it?

Puzzle No. 14

SET 1

Ageless age

'How old is Tina's father,' Rita wondered.

Nikita: 'Well, eighteen years ago he was three times as old as his son.'

'But now, it appears, he is only twice as old as his son,' said Rita.

Nikita tried to guess Tina's father's age, and his son's age. Time for you to guess now!

SET 2

Which number completes the puzzle?

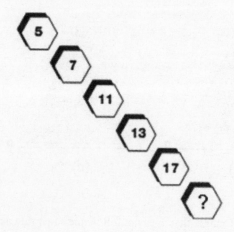

Puzzle No. 15

One grid in this sequence is missing. What should that be?

?

Puzzle No. 16

SET 1

Tina's googly

Tina can you find a number, which when added to itself one or many times gives a total having the same digits as that number, but when differently arranged, and after the sixth addition, gives a total of all 9s?

SET 2

Nikita's Prime Number quiz

Tina do you know which is the largest known Prime Number? *Do you?*

Puzzle No. 17

Find the letter that comes next down here and completes
the series?

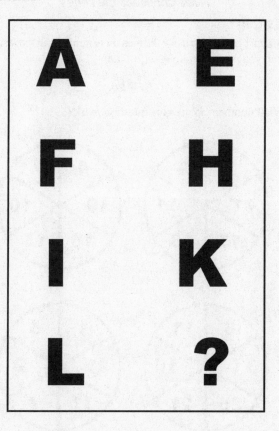

Puzzle No. 18

SET 1

Nikita continues the series

1, 3, 6, 10

Nikita, time now to name the next three numbers in the series.
Can you work this along with Tina?

SET 2

What number replaces the question mark?

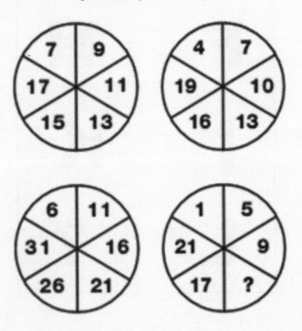

Puzzle No. 19

What is the logic behind these domino pieces? Also, fill in the missing letter?

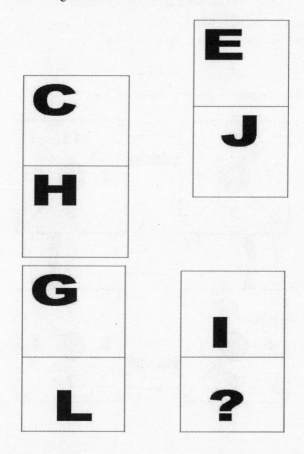

Puzzle No. 20

SET 1

Nikita has a probability problem

Hey Nikita, is it possible that there are 53 Tuesdays in a non-leap year? What is the probability?

SET 2

Which number replaces the question mark?

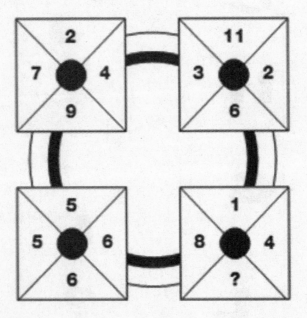

Puzzle No. 21

What is the logic behind these domino pieces? Also, fill in the missing digit?

5	3	8	7
12	15	49	56
3	9	4	12
18	27	36	?

Puzzle No. 22

SET 1

Tina's Probability: Tail or Head

Tina, what if six coins are flipped. What according to you is the probability of at least getting one tail?

SET 2

Nikita has a division problem

Nikita's uncle asked her to divide 1000 into two parts such that one part is a multiple of 47 and the other a multiple of 19? So what is the solution that Nikita got?

Puzzle No. 23

Can you work out the reasoning behind these trapezoids and replace the question mark with a number?

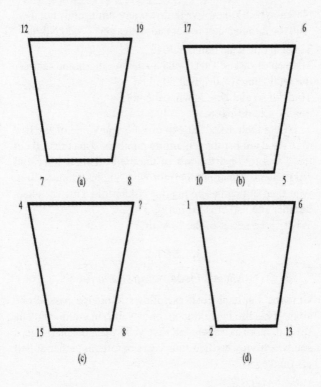

(a)

(b)

(c)

(d)

Puzzle No. 24

SET 1

Tina caught in the case of the missing digit

Nikita asked Tina to write down any multi digit number: 'But the number should not end with a zero,' said Nikita.

Tina put down the number 96452.

Then Nikita asked Tina to add up the five digits and subtract the total from the original number.

Tina did so and here is what she got:

96452 – 26 = 96426

Nikita then asked Tina to cross out any one of the five digits and tell her the remaining numbers. Tina crossed out the 2 and told her the rest of the digits. Tina neither told Nikita the original number nor what she had done with it. And then out came the magic! Nikita told Tina the exact number she had crossed out.

What is the secret of the MAGIC?

SET 2

Nikita's loses her grandfather

Grandpa's epitaph read as follows: Grandpa passed one sixth of his life in childhood, one twelfth in youth, and one seventh more as a bachelor. Five years after his marriage, a son was born who died four years before his father at half his final age

How old is Grandpa?

Puzzle No. 25

What is the logic behind these domino pieces? Also, fill in the missing letter?

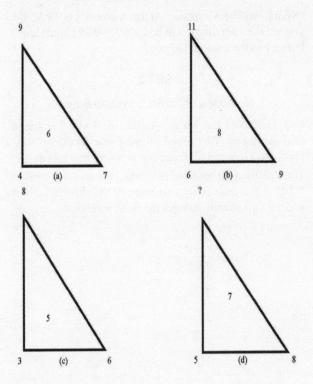

Puzzle No. 26

SET 1

Nikita meets Grandpa clock!

'Nikita,' said her Grandpa. 'At this moment it is 9 P.M. Can you tell me what time it will be 23999 999 992 hours later?' Nikita had the answer. Do you?

SET 2

Notebook of Nikita: Lost and Found

One day Nikita lost her new notebook. Two other friends also lost theirs. Tina found all the three. But there was a problem. They had all forgotten to write their names.

Tina returned the books to Nikita and the others at random. What is the probability that none of the three i.e. Nikita and the two friends will get the right notebook?

Puzzle No. 27

Complete the series by finding the missing number.

3 4 6 8 9 12 15 16 ?

Puzzle No. 28

SET 1

Nikita and Tina's problem of gifts

It was Christmas. A day to exchange gifts. Both their parents gave their respective daughters some money. Nikita received ₹150/- and Tina ₹100/-. But when the two of them counted their money, they found that between them they had become richer by only ₹150/-

Wonder how? How do you explain this?

SET 2

What's in a name…

Nikita—the name matters! What is the name given to the series?

0,1,1,2,3,5,8,13,21,34,55 ?

Puzzle No. 29

What is the logic behind these domino pieces? Also, fill in the missing letter?

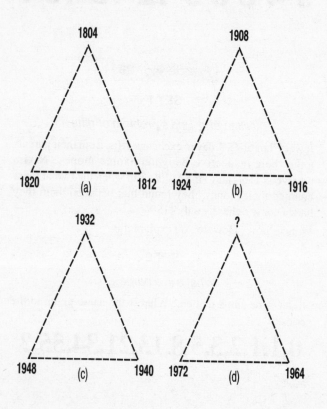

Puzzle No. 30

SET 1

Nikita wants the value of 'T' in TINA

T434S0 : What number must there be instead of 'T' to make it divisible by 36?

SET 2

Examination paper of Nikita and Tina

Is there a largest pair of twin primes?

Is there always at least one prime between two successive perfect squares?
Is there a largest even perfect number?

Puzzle No. 31

What is the logic behind these domino pieces? Also, fill in the missing letter?

Puzzle No. 32

SET 1

Nikita visits Rome

In Rome, Nikita went to a museum and saw this written below a statute: MDCLX VI

What year does it represent?

SET 2

Nikita returns home from Rome

Tina has a problem. She wants Nikita to write 1789 in Roman figures. Guess what does it look like!

SET 3

A New Year Party

It was the 31st of December; it was New Year's Eve. And on this day Nikita's family decided that her whole family should meet. The gathering consisted of one grandfather, one grandmother, two fathers, two mothers, four children, three grandchildren, one brother, two sisters, two sons, two daughters, one father-in-law, one mother-in-law, and one daughter-in-law. They were altogether seven.

Tina how do you explain it?

Puzzle No. 33

Just find the missing letter and complete this diagram?

B	P	?	F
D	N	T	D
F	L	V	B
H	J	X	Z

Puzzle No. 34

SET 1

Father time meets Nikita and Tina

'Come on Nikita and Tina', growled Father Time. 'What does 1408 hours mean?'

SET 2

Which number replaces the question mark?

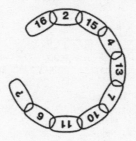

Puzzle No. 35

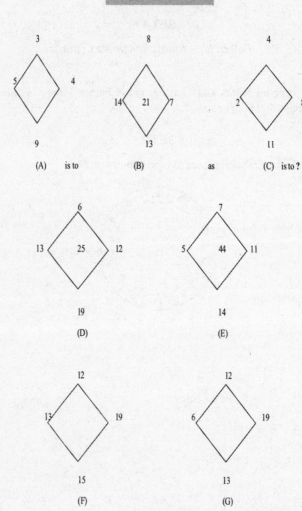

3

5   4

9

(A)   is to

8

14 21 7

13

(B)

as

4

2   8

11

(C) is to ?

6

13 25 12

19

(D)

7

5 44 11

14

(E)

12

13   19

15

(F)

12

6   19

13

(G)

Puzzle No. 36

SET 1

Tina, Nikita, Barbie and Ken are at their monthly business meeting. Their occupations are author, biologist, chemist and doctor, but not necessarily in that order. Ken just told the biologist that Barbie was on her way with doughnuts. Tina is sitting across from the doctor and next to the chemist. The doctor was thinking that Nikita was a goofy name for parent's to choose, but didn't say anything. What is each person's occupation?

SET 2

Which number replaces the question mark?

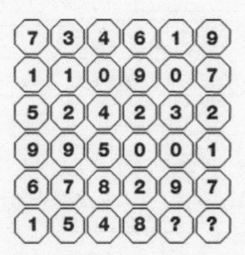

Puzzle No. 37

Time now to crack your brain and replace the question mark.

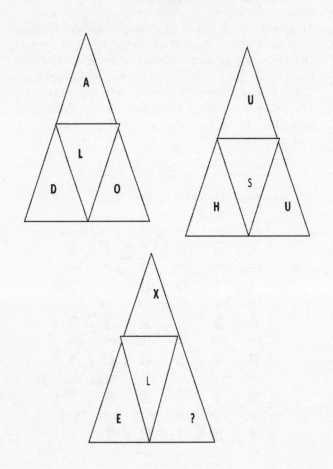

Puzzle No. 38

SET 1

Tina is about to find out the sequences

What are the next terms in the sequence?

17, 15, 26,22,35, 29, ... How about you?

SET 2

Nikita finds out five terms of another series

These are the numbers that are the first five terms of a series that add upto 150. Tina can do so.

Can you name five terms of another series, without fractions, that add upto 153?

10, 20, 30, 40, 50.

Puzzle No. 39

Time now for you to replace the question mark with a number?

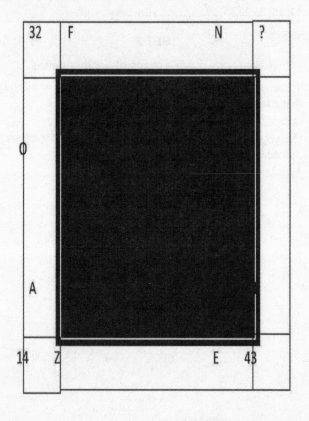

Puzzle No. 40

SET 1

Knitting needles of Nikita and Tina

Tina's has 'size 16' knitting needle twice as thick as Tina's 'size 8' knitting needle?

SET 2

A Problem of chain letters

Nikita opened her mail box this morning. What did she see in it? A chain letter.

She began to wonder. If one person sends a certain letter to two friends, asking each of them to copy the letter and send it to two of their friends, those in turn each send two letters to two of their friends and so on how many letters would have been sent by the time the letter did thirty sets.

She calculated and she was really surprised… the answer was gigantic. Let us check it out for ourselves!

Puzzle No. 41

Get working and find the missing number?

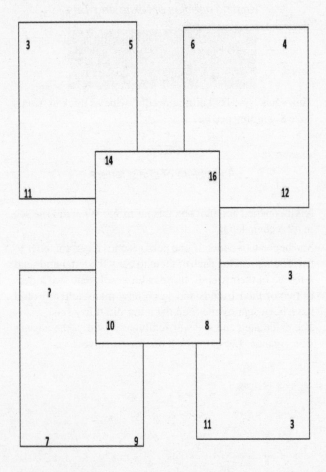

Puzzle No. 42

SET 1

Missing terms

Tina had a question for Nikita:

48, 60, 58, 72, 68, 104

Here is a sequence, she said. Can you find the two missing terms?

SET 2

Measure out the Time

Nikita has an old grandpa clock at home. It takes seven seconds for this clock to strike seven gongs. Now how long do you think it will take to strike ten gongs?

SET 3

Return gifts for Nikita's Birthday Party

6 men could pack 6 packets of candy in 6 minutes. She wondered how many men were required to pack 60 packets in 60 minutes. What do you think is the answer?

Puzzle No. 43

Can you find the missing letter?

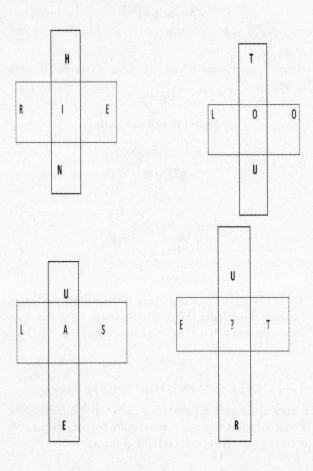

Puzzle No. 44

Can you spot the odd one out in the bottom triangle?

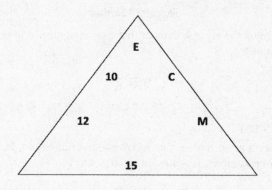

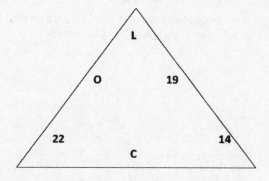

Puzzle No. 45

Nikita's three questions

SET 1

Biggest Number

What is the biggest number that can be expressed in three figures?

SET 2

Find Out

1757051

Take a good look at this number. Now tell Nikita, is it a prime number? If not, what are its factors?

SET 3

Mnemonic

'May I have a large container of coffee.' This is a mnemonic. Can you tell what is signifies?

Puzzle No. 46

Time now for you to find out which number should replace the question mark?

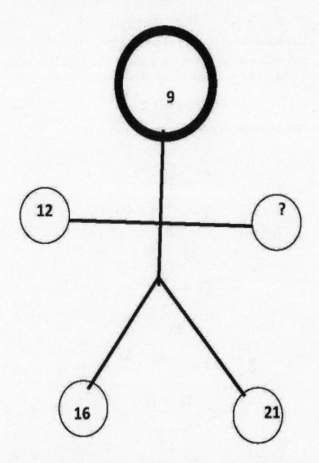

Puzzle No. 47

A problem of ribbon

SET 1

Tina's question

Tina has a 100 m piece of ribbon.

If it takes one second to cut it into a 1 m strip, how long would it take to cut the entire ribbon into metre strips?

SET 2

Which number is the odd one out in each oval?

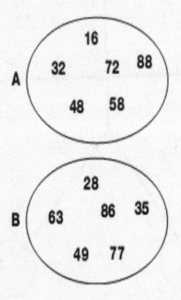

Puzzle No. 48

Take a look at this and find out which are the two odd letters out in these triangles?

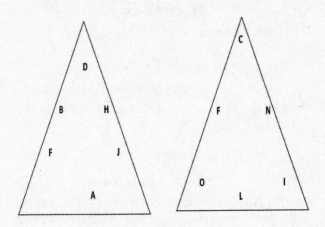

Puzzle No. 49

Nikita questions

SET 1

Value of a Googol

How much is a googol?

SET 2

Angle of Hands

The time is 2.15 P.M. What is the angle between the hour and minute hands?

SET 3

A problem of candy bars

Recently Nikita attended a birthday party. All the children in the party were given candy bars. All the children got three candy bars each except the child sitting in the end. She got only two candy bars. If only each child had been given two candy bars there would have been eight candy bars remaining. How many candy bars were there altogether to begin with?

Puzzle No. 50

Take a look at this figure and find the missing number in this wheel?

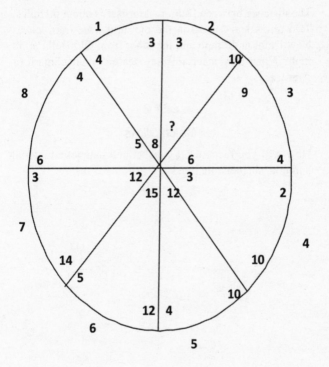

Puzzle No. 51

SET 1

Speeding Train

The distance between Delhi to Amritsar is about 60 miles. Two trains leave at 10 in the morning. One train leaves New Delhi at 40 mph and the other from Old Delhi at 50 mph. When they meet are they nearer to Chandigarh or Amritsar?

SET 2

Match Sticks

How will you recognise a magnet and magnetic material and non-magnetic material?

Puzzle No. 52

Now, find the odd number out?

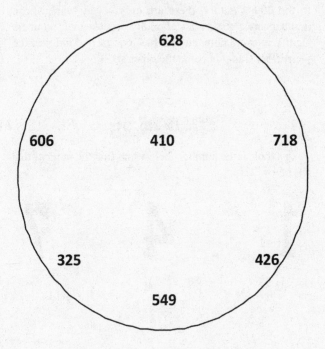

Puzzle No. 53

Mathematical Oddity

In the 20th Century, there are only seven years whose numbers are a mathematical oddity because their numbers signify a prime number. The first one of its kind was the year 1951. Can you name the other six?

Puzzle No. 54

Take a look at the numbers below and find the number that fits below 7?

1   4   7

32   41   ?

Puzzle No. 55

SET 1

The Problem of the Music Concert

Recently Tina was at a music concert in Berlin. Tina was sitting only one hundred feet away from the musicians.

The performance was being broadcasted. Her sister Nikita who lives in Munich also heard the same concert on the radio.

Do you think there was any difference in the times at which the music was heard by Tina and Nikita? If so, which one of them heard the note first?

SET 2

Which number replaces the question mark?

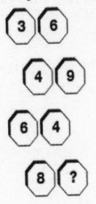

Puzzle No. 56

SET 1

Classify the numbers

Here are a set of numbers says NIKITA:

161 163 167 169 187

289 293 365 367 371

Can you classify these numbers as prime numbers and composite numbers. And when you find a composite number, can you give its prime factors?

SET 2

A Problem of Weight

In Nikita's neighborhood lives a man who weighs 200 kilos. He has two sons. They both weight 100 kilos each. On festival day, they decide to go across the river on a boat to visit some relations. But the boat could carry a maximum load of only 200 kilos.

Yet they managed to get across the river by boat. How did they?

Puzzle No. 57

SET 1

Height of a Room

Given the floor area of a room as 24 feet by 48 feet, and the space diagonal of the room as 56 feet, can you find the height of the room?

SET 2

Two candles of equal lengths and of different thickness are there. The thicker one will last for six hours. The thinner 2 hours less than the thicker one. Ramesh lights the two candles at the same time. When he went to bed he saw the thicker one is twice the length of the thinner one. For how long did Ramesh lit two candles?

Puzzle No. 58

Multiply the missing number by 4 and subtract 3 to find the passcode to your next puzzle. Start at 28.

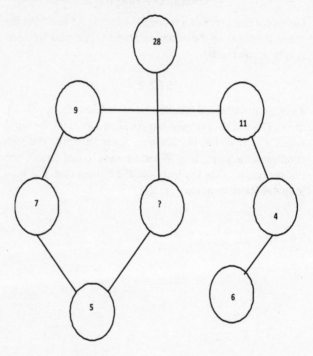

Puzzle No. 59

SET 1

Average Speed

It was a long drive. Tina drove 60 kilometres at 30 kilometres per hour and then an additional 60 kilometres at 50 kilometres per hour.

Compute Tina's average speed over 120 kiometres.

SET 2

A Problem of Water Lillies

In India, water lilies grow extremely rapidly in the ponds. If the growth enlarged so much that each day it covered a surface double than which it filled the day before, so that at the end of the 20th day it entirely covered the pond, in which it grew, how long would it take two water lilies of the same size at the outset and at the same rate of growth to cover the same pond?

SET 3

Which number replaces the question mark?

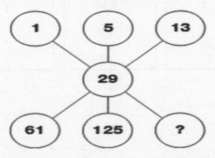

Puzzle No. 60

Continue the sequence (left to right) and deduct 34 from the missing number to find your next passcode.

72	64	57

51	46	?

Puzzle No. 61

SET 1

Decode the Mnemonic

Here is a piece of Mnemonic:
Now I - even I, would celebrate
In rhymes unapt the great
Immortal syracusan rivaled never more,
who in his wondrous lore
Passed on before,
Left men his guidance
How to circles mensurate.
Can you tell what it signifies?

SET 2

Which number down here replaces the question mark?

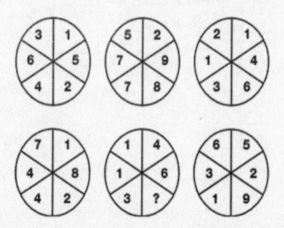

Puzzle No. 62

Look at A, B and C to find your next passcode.

A
A
B
B
C
36

A
B
B
B
C
38

A
A
A
B
C
34

A
B
C
C
C
28

A
B
C
?

Puzzle No. 63

SET 1

A Problem of Family Relations

Every man or woman alive today had 2 parents, 4 grandparents, 8 great-grandparents, 16 great-great-grandparents, 32 great, great, great grandparents and so on.

Let us take the case of Nikita. Two generations ago Nikita had 2 x 2 or 22, or 4 ancestors. Three generations ago she had 2 x 2 x 2 or 2 or 8 ancestors. Four generations ago she had 2 x 2 x 2 x 2 or 2 or 16 ancestors.

Assuming that there are 20 years to a generation, can you tell 400 years back, how many ancestors did Nikita have?

SET 2

Counting a billion

If you were to count one number per second and counted seven hours per day, how long would it take you to count to a billion?

SET 3

A Question of Identity

Is this a prime number?
1000009

Puzzle No. 64

This square has eleven letters missing that you have to replace. Just remember, every row, column and the main diagonals contain all the letters in the word 'Brave'.

B	R	A	V	E
	E	B	R	
		V		B
	B	R		
		E	B	

Puzzle No. 65

Given only one of each letter in the alphabet, what are the smallest and largest numbers that you could write down?

Puzzle No. 66

What letter of the alphabet is the one which comes nine letters before the letter, which comes three letters after the first letter to occur four times in this sentence?

Puzzle No. 67

The diagram below shows a cross-shaped box containing three numbered blocks. The puzzle is to slide the blocks around the box until the numbers read 1,2,3 as and when you go down. How do you do it?

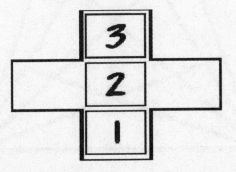

Puzzle No. 68

How many triangles and quadrilaterals are there in this diagram?

Puzzle No. 69

Nikita was looking through the family photograph album, which has a photo of each of her parent, each of her grandparents... each of her great-great-great-grandparents. So how many photos does it have in total?

Puzzle No. 70

Six boys catch six butterflies in six minutes.

How many boys will be needed to catch sixty butterflies in sixty minutes?

Puzzle No. 71

Nikita was playing with her building bricks when she made a tower like the one as you see below. So how many blocks did Nikita use eventually?

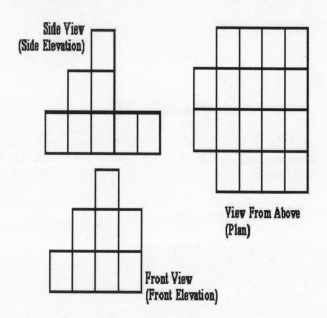

Side View
(Side Elevation)

View From Above
(Plan)

Front View
(Front Elevation)

Puzzle No. 72

If Nikita had six matches, it would be easy to make two identical triangles.

Now Tina has got to take six matches and make 4 similar triangles.

Time for you to help Tina do that!

Remember, the matches don't have to be the same length.

Puzzle No. 73

If you continue shading the squares so that the two dotted lines become lines of a mirror of the completed diagram, how many squares will be left unshaded?

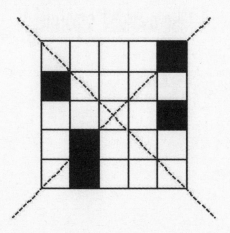

Puzzle No. 74

 This is Tina's favourite type of chocolate.

She went to the shop to buy one, but found that the chocolates had been packed up in boxes of three like this:

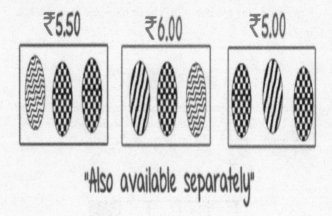

"Also available separately"

How much does Nikita's favourite chocolate cost?

Puzzle No. 75

Eight squares of paper, all exactly the same size, have been placed on top of each other so that they overlap as shown. In what order were the sheets placed?

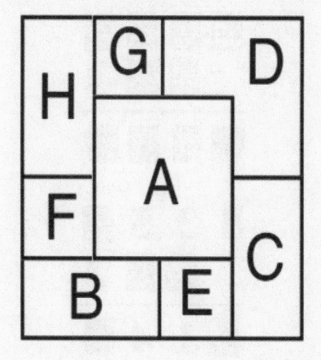

Puzzle No. 76

Time now to solve this puzzle. The idea is that each type of block stands for a different number, but that this number is the same wherever that sticker occurs.

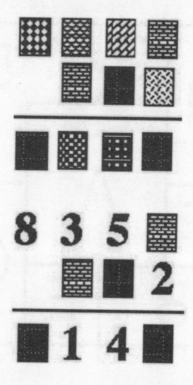

Puzzle No. 77

According to Nikita, in three days' time it would be a Thursday. Which means today is a Monday!

Now Nikita asks you this: Yesterday was two days before Monday. What day is it today? It's Sunday!

Now here is what Tina asks:

Three days ago, yesterday was the day before Sunday. Which is?

Puzzle No. 78

Nikita caught a cold. Fortunately, she did manage to get a message through Tina. Naughty Tina has hidden the message in a mysterious code. Time to crack the code.

PYNEWYE
PASEVEA
AMRRYRR
HTEMCYT
ASIRHBO
DNAYDOO

Puzzle No. 79

An old history puzzle book contained this addition sum which had been marked correct by the high priest:

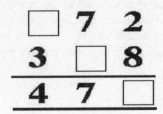

Find out the three missing numbers?

Puzzle No. 80

Using three straight lines, divide the circles patch up into six sections with two circles in each section.

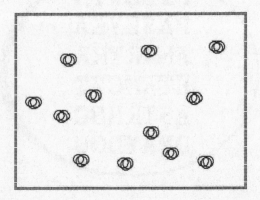

ANSWERS

Puzzle No. 1

QUS 2321.

To calculate each plate, go forward by 4, back by 2 in the alphabet to get the 2nd and 3rd letters. Continue this pattern, but use numbers representing the letters' alphabetical position.

Puzzle No. 2

1. Nikita's purchases cost ₹9.60.
2. There is nothing to explain here. The driving time there and back is absolutely the same because 90 minutes and 1 hour and 30 minutes are one and the same thing.

Puzzle No. 3

B. The digits of all the others add up to 6.

Puzzle No. 4

1. The smallest integer that can be written with two digits is not 10 as one may assume. But it is expressed as follows:

    1/1, 2/2, 3/3, 4/4 etc Upto 9/9

2. People often think of the number 1111 as the biggest number that can be written with four 1s. But there is a number many, many times greater than this number, namely: 11(11)

   11(11) = 285311670611

   11(11) is almost 250 million times greater than 1111.

   3. (150 − 1) = 149, since all, but one lose one game.

Puzzle No. 5

Yellow-Red-Green and Blue-Blue-Green and Yellow-Green-Yellow.

Puzzle No. 6

1 This problem can be solved only by application of algebra. Supposing we take X for the years, the age three years, hence will be X + 3 and the age three years ago X − 3. Now we have the equation 3(X + 3) − 3(X − 3) = X. When we solve this, we obtain: 18. The girl is 18 years old.

1. One can think of at least 9 examples:

   $39 \times 186 = 7254$

   $18 \times 297 = 5349$

   $28 \times 157 = 4396$

   $42 \times 138 = 5796$

   $12 \times 483 = 5796$

   $48 \times 159 = 7632$

   $4 \times 1738 = 6952$

   $27 \times 198 = 5346$

   $4 \times 1963 = 7852$

   If you try patiently, perhaps you may come up with some more.

Puzzle No. 7

Kebab, Pasta, Pizza, Tacos, Wurst.

Puzzle No. 8

1. 0123456789...
2. $22 + 2 + 1 = 25$

Puzzle No. 9

384. Starting at the top right-hand corner, work through the square vertically, multiplying by 4 and dividing by 2 alternately.

Puzzle No. 10

1. $888 + 88 + 8 + 8 + 8 = 1000$
2. 31

Puzzle No. 11

V. The letters are based on the number alphabetic backwards ($Z = 1$, $A = 26$, etc). The values on the bottom corners and the value in the middle, added together, result in the value on the apex.

Puzzle No. 12

1. $S = 112 + 126 + \ldots\ldots\ldots\ldots\ldots\ldots\ldots 994$
   $S = 14(8 + 9 + \ldots\ldots\ldots\ldots\ldots\ldots\ldots 71)$

2.

Puzzle No. 13

C. Divide the left number by 2, place this number at the apex, then square it and put this number at the right. Finally, add all three numbers together and put the sum as a Roman numeral in the middle. In triangle C, the right number should be 4 and the middle number should be X.

Puzzle No. 14

1. If the son is X years old, then the Father is 2x years old. Eighteen years ago they were both eighteen years younger. The father was 2x – 8 and the son x – 18. We know that then the father was three times as old as the son:
   3(x – 18) = 2x – 18
   When we solve this equation, we will find that x = 36. The son is 36 and the father 72.
2. 19. As you move down diagonally, the sequence is that of prime numbers.

Puzzle No. 15

	0	
	X	

Starting at opposite ends, the symbols move alternately 1 and 2 steps to the other end of the grid.

Puzzle No. 16

1. 142857
2. $2(127-1)$ = 170 141 83460469231731687303715884
   105 727

Puzzle No. 17

M. These are all the letters with straight sides only.

Puzzle No. 18

1. 15, 21, 28. These are triangular numbers: 1, 3, 6, 10,

   15, 21, 28........ $\dfrac{n(n+1)}{2}$

2. 13. In each circle, starting at the top left segment, numbers increase, as you move clockwise, by 2 for the upper left circle, 3 for the upper right, 4 for the lower right and 5 for the lower left.

Puzzle No. 19

N. going from the top to the bottom of one domino piece, then to the top of the next piece, etc., alternately move on five letters and three back.

Puzzle No. 20

1. 1/ 7. $52 \times 7 = 364 + 1 = 365$ days. There is a probability of anyone day of the week occurring; in a non – leap year it is one – seventh.
2. 9. In each square of the diagram, the sum of the numbers is always.

Puzzle No. 21

48. In each box of four numbers, multiply the top two numbers, put the product in the bottom right box, then subtract the top right number from the bottom right one and put the difference in the bottom left box.

Puzzle No. 22

1. $(2^6 - 1) / 2^6 = \dfrac{63}{64}$

2. $(18 \times 19) + (14 \times 47) = 1000$

Puzzle No. 23

The numbers rotate anti-clock wise from one square to the next and decrease by 2 each time.

Puzzle No. 24

1. Very simple. All you have to do is to find the digit which, added to the two you will get nearest divisible by 9. For example, in 639, cross out the 3, and consider the other two 6 and 9. Add them and get 15. The nearest number divisible by 9 is 18. Therefore the missing number is 3.
2. Let us assume a is Grandpa's age
    $a / 6 + a / 12 + a / 7 + 5 + a / 2 + 4 = a; a = 84$
    Grandpa's lived to be 84-years-old.

Puzzle No. 25

10. Add 2 to each value, place the sum in a corresponding position in the next triangle, then subtract 3, add 2 again.

Puzzle No. 26

1. 24 billion hours later it would be 9 o'clock and 8 hours before that it would be one o'clock.

2. We shall do a simple listing below, which will provide us the solution:

1	2	3	Conditions Met
1	2	3	No
1	3	2	No
2	1	1	No
2	3	1	Yes
3	1	2	Yes
3	2	1	No

Answer is 2 / 6 or 1 / 3

Puzzle No. 27

18. These are all the numbers that can be divided by either 3 or 4.

Puzzle No. 28

1. One of the parents is the daughter of the other parent. The problem posed would seem as if there are altogether four persons concerned. But that is not so. The three persons are Nikita who gave her daughter ₹150/- and the latter passed ₹100/ Tina (i.e. her daughter). Thus increasing her own money by ₹50/-.

2. This series is called the Fibonacci series wherein the sum of the 2nd and 3rd terms equal the 4th, the sum of the 3rd and 4th term equals the 5th term, the sum of the 4th and 5th term equals the 5th term....

Puzzle No. 29

1956. The numbers represent the leap years clockwise around the triangles starting at the apex. Miss one leap year each time.

Puzzle No. 30

1. If T434S0 is to be divisible by 36, then it is also divisible by 4 and 9. To be divisible by 4, S must be an even number. To be divisible by 9, 25 + 11 is a multiple of 9. The digit '8' is the only number that meets these two conditions. When we substitute 'S' with '8' we get the answer.
    843480.
2. No one knows!

Puzzle No. 31

F. This is based on the number alphabet backwards. Add together the corner squares of each row or column and put the sum in the middle square of the opposite row or column.

Puzzle No. 32

1. M = 1000   D = 500   C = 100
    L = 50   X = 10 and VI = 6
    If we add all these together, the result is 1666.
2. M D C C L X X X I X
3. There were two girls and a boy, their father and mother, and their father's father and mother. As it would be too much for words to go into the explanations of relationships here, the most satisfactory thing for you to do would be to sit down, write out a list of the seven people involved, and check off the twenty three relationships.

Puzzle No. 33

R. Starting on the top left hand corner, work through the alphabet, missing a letter each time, vertically.

Puzzle No. 34

1. The time is 8 minutes past 2 P.M.
2. 16. Moving clockwise, around alternate segments in the chain, one sequence decreases by 1, 2, 3 and 4 each time, while the other increases by 2, 3, 4 and 5.

Puzzle No. 35

D. Add consecutive clockwise corners of the diamond and place the sum on the corresponding second corner. Add the four numbers together and place the sum in the middle.

Puzzle No. 36

1. Since Ken spoke to the biologist and Tina sat next to the chemist and across the doctor, Barbie must be the author and Tina the biologist. The doctor didn't speak, but Ken did, so Nikita is the doctor and Dave the chemist.
2. 8,1. Reading each row as 3 separate 2-digit numbers, the central number equals the average of the left and right hand numbers.

Puzzle No. 37

Y. It spells Aldous Huxley.

Puzzle No. 38

1. 44, 36 – The odd terms increase by 9 each time, and the even terms increase by 7 each time.
2. Each terms in this series is a factorial. The first five terms of the series are, therefore 1, 2, 6, 24, 120 and the sum of these number is 153.

Puzzle No. 39

83. Add the values of the letters in each box, based on the alphabet backwards (i.e Z = 1, a = 26) and place the sum, with the digits reversed, two squares ahead.

Puzzle No. 40

1. No. Knitting needles conform to the Standard Wire Guage (S.W.G.) sizes, and the larger the S.W.G. numbers, the smaller is the diameter of the wire.
2. The thirteenth set would consist of:
   2^{30} = 1073 74 1824 letters.
   The first set consist of 2 letters.
   The second set consist of 4 letters.
   The third set consists of 8 letters.
   And therefore, the 30th set would consist of 2^{30} letters.

Puzzle No. 41

Add the two top outer numbers from the upper boxes and the two bottom numbers from the lower box and put the sum in the inner box diagonally opposite the third outer number is obtained by subtracting 3, 4, 5, and 6 from the adjoining answer, starting from the top left and reading clockwise. The answer is obtained as follows: 6 + 4 (top right's two outer top number) = 10 (bottom left's inner numbers) - 6 = 4.

Puzzle No. 42

1. 78, 116 The odd terms are in the decimal system and differ by 10. And each even term is the preceding odd term expressed in the octonary system. $78 - 8 = 9$, remainder $6 : 9 : 8 = 1$, remainder 1.
2. $(7 / 16) \times 9 + 10\frac{1}{2}$ seconds
3. 6 men pack 6 boxes in 6 minutes
   6 men pack 1 box in 1 minutes
   6 men pack 60 box in 60 minutes.

Puzzle No. 43

C. It spells Henri Toulouse Lautrec.

Puzzle No. 44

1. Each letters has a partner in the other triangle, which is its value in the alphabet backwards (A = 26, Z = 1). The number equivalent for C should be 24 (the letter for 3 is x).

Puzzle No. 45

1. The product of 387420489 9s!
2. It is not a prime number. $1767051 \times 1291 \times 1361$
3. The value of Pi to seven places of decimals are contained in this mnemonic. The numbers of letters in each word corresponds to the successive integers in the decimal expansion of Pi.

Puzzle No. 46

27. The numbers increase by 3, 4, 5, 6 in an anti-clockwise direction.

Puzzle No. 47

1. One minute and thirty nine seconds, because when the ninety ninth cut is made, the remaining metre does not have to be cut.
2. A:58 B:86. In the first oval, all numbers are multiples of 8, and in the second, they are all multiples of 7.

Puzzle No. 48

A and **N.** The series is B, D, F, H, J (2, 4, 6, 8, 10). Add 1, 2, 3, 4, 5 respectively to the values to get the letters in the second triangle.

Puzzle No. 49

1. The googol is : 10,000, 000, 000, 000, 000, 000,000, 000, 000, 000, 000, 000, 000, 000, 000, 000, 000, 000, 000, 000, 000, 000, 000, 000, 000, 000, 000, 000, 000, 000, 000, 000.
2. 22½°. The hour moves same fraction of the distance between two and three (30°) as the minute hand has moved of a complete rotation (¼).

$$30 - 1/4\ (30) = 30 - 7\frac{1}{2} = 22\ \frac{1}{2}$$

3. If there were x children at the party then the two ways of distributing the candy can be represented by these two expressions:
   $3(x - 1) + 2$ and $2x + 8$
   Therefore $3x - 3 + 2 = 2x + 8$
   Or $x = 9$
   The number of candy for distribution $= 2 \times 9 + 8$
   $= 26$

Puzzle No. 50

10. Multiply the two numbers on the outside of each segment, divide the product by 1, 2.

Puzzle No. 51

1. The train leaving Amristar travels faster, and naturally they meet and cross one another nearer to Delhi . The meeting place is 40 / 90 of 60 or 26 – 2/3 miles from Delhi and 50 / 90 of 60 or 33 – 1/3 miles from Delhi, and this happens at 10 – 40 A.M.

2. Drag one piece of material over another. There is no attractive force in the middle portion of the magnet. Or get a piece of thread and tie up with the one bar and check for poles. If it is an iron bar then it moves freely and if it is a magnetic bar then it gets fixed in one direction according to the poles.

Puzzle No. 52

410. In all the others the first two digits added results in the third digit.

Puzzle No. 53

1.   1973, 1979, 1987, 1993, 1997, 1999

Puzzle No. 54

11. Multiply the number of sides of each number by 3, and then subtract the number printed.

Puzzle No. 55

1.   Nikita did. The person listening to the radio hears the given note first.
2.   1. Reading each pair of numbers as a 2 digit number, they follow the sequence of square numbers from 6 to 9.

Puzzle No. 56

1.	Primes	Composites
	163	$161 = 7 \times 23$
	167	$169 = 13^2$
	293	$187 = 11 \times 17$
	367	$289 = 17^2$

2. First, the two sons rowed across the river and one stayed behind while the other returned in the boat to his father. The son remained behind while the father crossed the river. Then the other son brought back the boat and the two brothers rowed over together.

Puzzle No. 57

1. Suppose x is the diagonal of the floor, then
   $x^2 = 24^2 + 48^2$, $x = 24\sqrt{5}$
   And if h is the height of the room, then
   $h^2 + (24\sqrt{5})^2 = 56^2$ and $h = 16$.
   Thus the height of the room is 16 ft.
2. 3 hours

Puzzle No. 58

45. The missing number is 12. With double digits, add both digits together and add 2 to get the next number. Thus, $2 + 8 = 10$, $10 + 2 = [12]$; $1+2 = 3$, $3 + 2 = 5$; $5 + 2 = 7$; $7 + 2 = 9$; $9 + 2 = 11$; $1+1 = 2$, $2+2 = 4$; $4 + 2 = 6$. $12 \times 4 = 48$; $48 - 3 = 45$. Go to 45.

Puzzle No. 59

1. Time required for the first sixty miles: 120 minutes
   Time required for the second sixty miles: 72 minutes.

Total time required: 192 minutes
I travelled 120 miles in 192 minutes. Therefore, the average speed in miles per hour was 60 × 120 / 192 = 37½

2. 19 days.
3. 253. Starting at the top left, and moving through the diagram in a Z shape, double each number and add 3 to give the next number along.

Puzzle No. 60

8. The missing number is 42. The sequence is a series of subtractions, reducing by 1 with each step. Thus, 72 – 8 = 64; 64 – 7 = 57; 57 – 6 = 51; 51 – 5 = 46; 46 – 4 = 42. 42 – 34 = 8. Go to 8.

Puzzle No. 61

1. Pi to 30 decimal places.
2. **7.** Taking the top row of circles, numbers in the central circle equal the sum of the numbers in corresponding segments of the left and right hand circles. In the bottom row, numbers in the central circle equal the difference between numbers in corresponding segments of the left and right hand circles.

Puzzle No. 62

1. **20.** A = 7; B = 9; C = 4. Go to 20

Puzzle No. 63

1. 1048576 – 400 years ago, that is 20 generations back, Nikita – for that matter each one of us had 2^{20} or 1048576 ancestors.
2. About 109 years.
3. No. 1000009 = 203 × 3413.

Puzzle No. 64

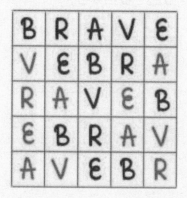

Puzzle No. 65

Using only one of each letter in the alphabet, you can spell:

ZERO or NOUGHT

MINUS TWO (allowing negative numbers)

FIVE THOUSAND

These are the smallest and largest possible numbers.

Puzzle No. 66

The alphabet is 'n'. You get this by working backwards through the puzzle: the first letter to occur four times is t, three letters after that is w and nine letters before that is n.

Puzzle No. 67

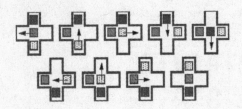

Puzzle No. 68

64 Triangles
36 Quadrilaterals
Total: 100 shapes

Puzzle No. 69

2   parents
4   grandparents
8   great-grandparents
16   great-great-grandparents
32   great-great-great-grandparents
   2 + 4 + 8 + 16 + 32 = 62 photos in all.

Puzzle No. 70

Each boy catches 1 butterfly in six minutes. In 60 minutes, therefore, each butterfly will catch 10 butterflies (ten times as many). With 6 boys, six times as many butterflies will be caught.

Puzzle No. 71

22 blocks in all!

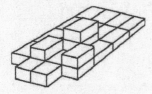

Puzzle No. 72

Or

Puzzle No. 73

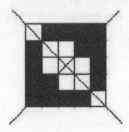

The number of squares left is then 9.

Puzzle No. 74

₹2.50

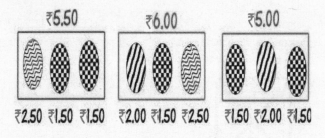

Puzzle No. 75

The paper squares were placed in this order: CEBFHGDA

Puzzle No. 76

The only numbers, which haven't been used so far are 0, 6, 7, and 9. The first one to work out is the brick wall, which has to be 7, since none of the others fit, which means the shaded square is 9, and the completed puzzle is:

$8357 + 792 = 9149.$

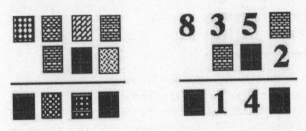

Puzzle No. 77

Three days ago, yesterday was the day before Sunday, so three days ago was itself Sunday.

That means today is Wednesday, so tomorrow is Thursday!

Puzzle No. 78

Merry Christmas everybody and a Happy New Year too. Start at the middle and spiral outwards!

Puzzle No. 79

And here is how to solve this: Start with the 0 on the bottom (don't forget to carry the 1!). Working towards the left, the next one has to be 9 to make the total 16 (+1 = 17) so we carry another 1. That means the top left digit must be empty (or a zero):

Puzzle No. 80

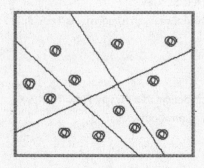